Droughts

Droughts

Patrick Merrick

THE CHILD'S WORLD®, INC.

Library of Congress Cataloging-in-Publication Data
Merrick, Patrick.
Droughts / by Patrick Merrick.
p.   cm.
Includes index.
Summary: Uses a question-and-answer format to provide
information about the causes of droughts, where they occur,
their characteristics, and the effects they produce.
ISBN 1-56766-470-9 (lib. bdg. : alk. paper)
1. Droughts—Juvenile literature.
[1. Droughts—Miscellanea. 2. Questions and answers.]   I. Title
QC929.25.M47   1998
551.57'73—dc21   97-28750
CIP
AC

Photo Credits

© 1996 A.B. Sheldon/Dembinsky Photo Assoc. Inc.: 10
© Bill Lea/Dembinsky Photo Assoc. Inc.: 6
© Charles McNulty/Tony Stone Images: 24
© Christopher Arnesen/Tony Stone Images: 26
© 1996 Darrell Gulin/Dembinsky Photo Assoc. Inc.: 13, 19
© Elizabeth Harris/Tony Stone Worldwide: 15
© 1997 John S. Botkin/Dembinsky Photo Assoc. Inc.: 20
© 1997 Martin Withers/Dembinsky Photo Assoc. Inc.: 9
© Mike & Carol Werner/Comstock, Inc.: 30
© Peter James Miller/AGStockUSA: 29
© Peter Pearson/Tony Stone Worldwide: 2
© 1997 Russ Gutshall/Dembinsky Photo Assoc. Inc.: 23
© 1997 Stan Osolinski/Dembinsky Photo Assoc. Inc.: cover
© 1993 Stan Osolinski/Dembinsky Photo Assoc. Inc.: 16

On the cover...

Front cover: This *mariposa lily* is trying to grow in the dried earth.
Page 2: Green grass is trying to grow in this dried-up pond.

Table of Contents

As the sun rises, the sky is blue and cloudless. Today looks as if it is going to be another beautiful day. It is hard to believe that a day like this could be the start of a natural disaster. What could such a disaster be? It is a drought (DROWT).

Most other natural disasters, such as tornadoes, lightning, and hurricanes, are fast and scary. But a drought is slow. It is simply a time when there is too little rain. Droughts can last from as little as three weeks to as long as a hundred years!

Without water, this African lake dried up. ⇒

Rain is how the land gets the water it needs. The land needs rain so plants can grow and animals can live. Rain also fills lakes and rivers and helps stop grass fires and forest fires. People need water, too. That's because our bodies are made mostly of water!

⇐ Rain showers like this one are very important.

Are There Different Types of Droughts?

There are two kinds of droughts. One kind of drought never stops. It is called a **permanent drought**. Areas with permanent droughts are usually called **deserts**. Deserts get less than eight inches of rain a year! Some famous deserts are the *Sahara Desert* in Africa and the *Gobi Desert* in Asia. There is also a large desert that can be found in the southwestern United States.

This desert in California rarely gets rain. ⇒

The other type of drought lasts from a few weeks to a few years. It is called a **contingent drought**. Contingent droughts can happen at any time. They cause a lot of damage, because no one is ready for them! Every part of the world experiences this kind of drought. Many plants, animals, and people can die during a contingent drought.

Plants and cracked mud are all that is left in this dried-up lake. ⇒

Where Do Droughts Happen?

Droughts can happen anywhere on Earth. They even happen in the United States. In 1996, there was a huge drought in the southwestern states. The ground became so dry that fires burned over 100,000 acres of trees. The farmers could not grow crops. Many cows and other animals starved because they had nothing to eat.

⇐ Forest fires like this one spread quickly in areas with droughts.

Droughts even affect people in big cities. In 1988, the water in California's rivers and lakes dropped very low. People were asked not to water their lawns or take long showers. Many restaurants and flower shops had to close—there was just too little water!

During a bad drought, this California pond dried up. ⇒

What Causes Droughts?

Droughts are caused by many different forces—the wind, the land itself, and even the ocean. Wind carries rain clouds all over the world. If the wind does not blow rain clouds over an area, there will be no rain. Mountains sometimes make a cloud's rain fall as the cloud moves up the mountain. This can cause the other side of the mountains to have a drought.

Even though the ocean is filled with water, it is one of the biggest causes of droughts. Within the ocean there are streams of moving water called **currents**. Two of these currents are **El Niño** and **El Niña**. El Niño is a current with very warm water. El Niña is a current that is very cold. When either current comes close to land, it causes problems. Too much rain falls in some areas, causing floods. Too little rain falls in other areas, causing droughts.

The ocean's currents keep most rain away from this African desert. ⇒

Are Droughts Dangerous?

Because everything needs water, droughts are very dangerous. Without rain, plants cannot grow. Sometimes people and animals cannot find enough food. That is called a **famine**. During a famine, people and animals become sick and even die from lack of food.

⬅ Without enough rain, the plants in this cornfield are dying.

One of the most famous droughts happened in the United States. During the 1930s, 10 states went through a terrible drought. They became known as the "Dust Bowl." Farmers lost almost all of their crops! Many of them had to sell their land and move to the city to try to find jobs and food.

The worst part of the drought was the dust storms. The wind would pick up the dry dirt and sweep it high into the air. These huge storms moved millions of tons of dirt and turned the sky as black as night. In Kansas alone, the drought and the dust storms killed 300,000 people!

⇐ This dust storm is much like those of the 1930s.

What Can People Do About Droughts?

Droughts are hard to stop, but some things can keep them from doing as much damage. Farmers can plant trees and bushes to keep the wind from blowing the dirt around. They can also plant their crops in ways that help save the soil.

These trees were planted to slow down the wind over this field. ⇒

Even people in the city can help fight droughts. We can all learn to save, or **conserve**, the water we already have. Watering the grass only in the early morning or evening helps to save water. So does shutting off the water when we are not using it. By saving water, we can help fight one of nature's worst disasters—the drought.

⇐ This wildflower is trying to grow in the dry earth.

Glossary

conserve (kun–SERV)
When you conserve something, you save it or use it carefully. It is important that we learn to conserve water.

contingent drought (kuhn–TIN–jent DROWT)
A contingent drought is one that lasts from a few weeks to a few years.

currents (KUR–entz)
Currents are large streams of water flowing within the ocean. Currents can cause changes in our weather, including droughts.

deserts (DEH–zerts)
Deserts are areas that get very little rain. There are deserts all over the world.

El Niña (el NEEN–yuh)
El Niña is a very cold stream of water in the ocean. It can cause weather changes, including floods and droughts, when it flows near land.

El Niño (el NEEN–yoh)
El Niño is a very warm stream of water in the ocean. Like El Niña, El Niño can cause droughts and floods when it flows close to land.

famine (FA–min)
A famine is a time when there is too little food. Droughts can sometimes cause famines.

permanent drought (PER–muh–nent DROWT)
A permanent drought is one that never ends. Many deserts have permanent droughts.

Index